very hard-working. He does all of his jobs very well and at the proper time, just as if he was a soldier in an army. Although he does not go to school like Omar, he successfully carries out the many tasks which he needs to do in his life.

You are wondering who this little friend is, aren't you?

Omar's secret friend is a little ant, who can do many wonderful things.

You may never have heard how skilful and intelligent ants are. Some of you may even think of them as simple insects that wander around all day without doing anything. But those of you who think like that are mistaken, because ants, just like many other living things, also have a life of their own.

Omar has the chance to learn about the details of this life from his friend. This is one of the reasons why he never fails to visit his friend and enjoys his chats with him so much.

Omar is very amazed by the things he learns from his friend about the world of the ants. He wants to share everything he learns about his little friend's talents, intelligence and all his other superior traits with other people.

What, then, makes Omar so excited? Why is he so fascinated by the world of ants? You must be wondering why. So just continue reading...

Ants have more of their own kind in this world than most other living creatures. For every 700 million ants that come into this world, there are only 40 newborn human beings. In other words, the number of ants in the world is way above the number of human beings.

Ant families are also very big. For instance, you probably have a family of 4-5 people. In an ant family, however, there are sometimes millions of ants. Now think for a minute: if you had millions of brothers and sisters, would you be able to live in a single house? Surely not!

The astonishing features of ants do not end here. Despite the fact that millions of them live together, they have no problems with each other, no mix-ups and no disorder. They live an extremely well planned life with everyone obeying the rules.

Some ant families do tailoring, others grow their own food like farmers, and yet others run small farms where they raise some smaller animals. In the same way as human beings breed cows and use their milk, ants breed small plant lice (aphids) and use their milk.

Now let's see what Omar has to say about the world of ants:

Weaver ants are skilful tailors. They combine leaves by pulling them from two sides and sewing the leaves together. In this way, they make a nice home for themselves.

Doorman ants guard the nest. They do this job very successfully. Other ants are also very hard-working. They do all the work of the nest.

Omar: I first noticed him when I saw his tiny head emerging from the earth. His head attracted my attention, as it was a bit bigger than his body. I wondered why his head was like that and started to watch this tiny friend of mine. The big head on his little body was helping him serve as a guard at the entrance of the nest. Do you want to know 'how?' He was checking whether the ants that attempted to enter the nest belonged to his own family or not, and did not let them in if they were strangers.

Soon after seeing him, I met him and asked him to tell me what was happening inside. My little friend understood my curiosity, and started to tell me about it. What I was wondering most was how the ants with big heads recognised their nest-mates and let them in.

The Ant: Omar, let me first tell you that we call our families a 'colony.' In other words, we live in communities called colonies. An ant can easily tell whether another ant belongs to its own colony or not. He does it by touching the other ant's body with his antenna, (thin little rods coming out of the top of his head) which helps him to distinguish strangers, thanks to the 'colony scent' they have. If the ant is a stranger, then we cannot let him into our home. Moreover, we may even have to use force to send him away.

Ants "talking" to one another by touching.

Ants do not want strangers to enter their nests, because this will threaten their security. They never hesitate to get into a fight to protect their nest and friends.

Omar was surprised to hear about their perfect security system and wondered how strangers that tried to enter the nest dared to do so. When he shared this thought with his friend, he smiled at him and said that there were many other things that would surprise him.

The Ant then said: "Let me tell now you about the inside of our nest, which you were eager to know about. Our colonies consist of the queen ant, male ants, soldiers, and worker ants.

Ants have different tasks. They all work very hard at their jobs without a moment's rest.

The queen and male ants keep our species going. The queen is larger than all of us. The duty of the males is to make the queen give birth to new ants. Soldiers are responsible for protecting our colony, hunting, and finding new places for nests. The last group consists of the worker ants. Worker ants are all sterile female ants.

That is, they cannot give birth to new ants. They take care of the queen and her babies, and clean and feed them. In addition, they also have to do all the other jobs in the colony. They build new corridors in the nest, search for food and clean the nest up. The worker and soldier ants also divide into smaller groups among themselves. Some of these are breeders, builders, and food-hunters. Each group has a different job. While one group fights off enemies or hunts, another group builds the nest, and yet another takes care of the cleaning and repairs of the nest."

As Omar's little friend explained all that, he listened to him with wonder, and then asked him: "Do you never get bored, waiting at the entrance of the nest all the time? What is your duty in the nest?"

The Ant replied: "I am also a worker, and my duty is to serve here as a doorman. As you see, my head is big enough to cover the entrance hole of the nest. I am pleased that I have this ability, and I carry out my duty with great pleasure. I never get bored; on the contrary, I am very glad that I protect friends from threats."

Hard-working workers on the job.

13

Omar couldn't help but be amazed at his answer. Ants were working all the time to help others, with no thought for themselves and without any problems—something even people cannot manage most of the time.

From what his little friend told him, he could easily understand that the work of the nest was perfectly divided up between the ants. It was obvious that the life of ants was very well-ordered and all the ants had to be quite unselfish. Then he wondered whether they had any fights amongst themselves because some of them claimed that they were better or stronger than others. His friend said that nothing like that ever happened and added:

"We are a big family, Omar. There is no jealousy, competition or ambition among us. We always help each other and do our best to serve the colony. Everything in the colony is based on sacrifice. Each ant thinks of the good of his friends first, and only then of himself. Let me give you an example. When

there is a shortage of food in the colony, the worker ants immediately change into 'feeder' ants, and start feeding others with the food in their reserve stomachs. When there is enough food in the colony, they again become worker ants.

I used to hear people saying that there is competition among living things in nature. Never believe what they say. We know very well that we have to cooperate to be successful."

Omar said that what he had told him about himself and his colony was a very good example of this. He was very glad to know that God had created him so unselfish, helpful and so fond of his friends. After what he told him, he decided to be at least as thoughtful of others as ants were, and be a good person whom God loves.

It had got quite late and he had to get to school. He told his friend that he had to go, but would certainly come to see him the next day.

The next day Omar went back to the same place and waited for his little friend. After a few minutes, he appeared. He told him that he had waited impatiently all night to see him again. Then he reminded him of his promise to tell him about the inside of the nest. So the ant started to tell him about his home:

"Although we are tiny animals, our nest is amazingly big, just like the headquarters of a big army. If you are a stranger, you can never get in. Because, as you already know, there are guards like me at the doors.

Inside, there is extremely orderly, non-stop activity. Thousands, even millions, of soldier and worker ants carry out their jobs in an organized way. Our buildings are very suitable for indoor work. There are special departments for each job, and these departments are designed in such a way that both the soldier ants and the worker ants like me can work in the easiest manner.

Besides, we consider all our needs while putting up our buildings. For instance, our building has floors underground which only let a limited amount of sunlight in. But there are also some departments where the sun's energy is needed. We build these departments on the top floors, which receive sunlight at the widest possible angle. And then again, there are departments that have to stay in constant touch with each other. We build these close to one another, so that the ants can

easily reach each other. Our storehouse, where the surplus materials are kept, is built as a separate department at one side of the building. The larders where we store our provisions are in places which are easy to reach. In addition to these, there is also a big hall right at the centre of the building where we gather on certain occasions."

At the side, we see an underground city built by ants. Despite their tiny size, they can, amazingly, build such big cities.

17

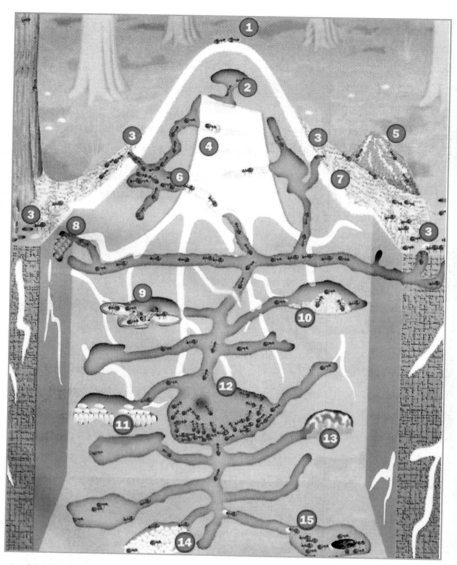

1. Air Defence System 2. Greenhouse 3. Main entrance and side entrances 4. Ready-made chambers 5. Storage cemetery 6. Guards' chamber 7. Outer shield 8. Nursing chamber 9. Meat depot 10. Grain depot 11. Childcare for larvae 12. Wintering room 13. Central heating department 14. Brooding room 15. Royalty room...

There is no doubt that ants cannot plan and devise all these details themselves. They are inspired by God to do so.

When Omar heard all that, he asked his little friend: "Do you really do all these things? I did not know that ants could work like skilful engineers and architects. If people are to build such perfect buildings, they have to spend many years at school and work very hard. Do you also receive such training?" In reply, the ant went on telling him of more mind-boggling things about his friends:

"No, Omar. All of us have these skills within us. These are never taught to us, but we know exactly

The house that ants build for themselves is almost like a castle for them.

19

what to do, and when. And that is not all. What I am going to tell you next will surprise you even more.

As I told you before, our building is very big compared to our size. In spite of this, however, it is heated evenly. In our nests, there is a very advanced central heating system. This way, the temperature stays constant all day long. To guarantee this, we cover the outside surface of our building with various materials that do not let the heat in. In this way, we prevent cold air getting in during the winter and keep hot air out in the summer. That is how we always keep the temperature at the same level."

There was no doubt that if Omar had not met his little friend, he would hardly have believed that ants could do all this. He said to the ant: "Before you told me all this, if someone had come up and told me about the

details of your nest and asked who could build a nest like that, I would have come up with very different answers. I would have said that such a nest could only be built with very fine tools and hard work by highly skilled people. If someone had told me that this building was not constructed by educated people but by ants, to tell you the truth, I would never have believed him."

While his little friend, the ant, was talking to him, many thoughts crossed his mind. He thought that they were more skilful than people, and started to see these animals differently. He understood that ants were created by God, and that it was God's inspiration at every moment that made them behave the way they did. Otherwise, they would never be able to do all these things successfully.

As all this was crossing his mind, his little

friend kept on speaking. As he went on, Omar grew even more interested, and wanted to ask him about everything that came to his mind. He asked the first question that occurred to him right away. He had earlier been told that ants behaved like farmers, so he asked him how they managed to do that. How could an ant, being so small, farm land without any tools, something that even a man could hardly do?

The Ant said: "Let me tell you one more thing about us. That way, it will be easier to answer your question. Although we all look very much alike, we are divided into many distinct groups according to the way we live and look. There are around 8,800 different kinds of ants. All the species have distinct features. The farmer ant is one of these species. Now, I will tell you about ants that engage in farming. They are called "attas", that is, leaf-cutting ants.

The foremost characteristic of attas is their habit of carrying on their heads the leaf pieces that they cut out. For this purpose, they first smooth out their path, so that they can easily move about on it. The road they travel to their nest while carrying the cut leaves looks like a small highway. Ants walk slowly along this path, collecting all the twigs, small bits of gravel, grass and wild plants on the ground, and removing them. Thus, they clear a path for themselves.

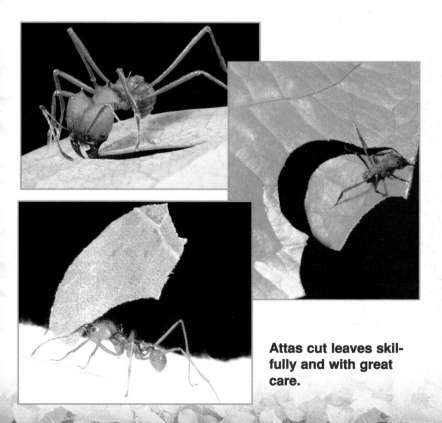

Attas cut leaves skilfully and with great care.

After much long and hard work, the highway becomes straight and smooth as if flattened by a special tool. Attas walk towards their nest on this path, hiding under big pieces of leaves, which they hold in their tightly clamped jaws."

Omar: Did you say they hide under leaves? Why do attas feel the need to hide under leaves?

The Ant: Attas have to be careful sometimes, Omar. For instance, medium-sized atta workers spend almost all day away from the nest, carrying leaves. It is difficult for them to protect themselves when they are doing that, because they carry the leaves in their jaws, which they normally use for self-defense.

Omar: So, if they are not able to protect themselves, who does it for them?

1- Ants chop the leaves they bring to the nest into bits.
2- They chew these bits into pulp.
3- They apply this pulp over a base of dried leaves in new chambers.
4- They place bits of fungus they take from other chambers over this pulp.
5- A busy group of ants cleans the garden and removes all unnecessary materials.

The Ant: Leaf cutter worker ants are always accompanied by smaller workers. These workers climb on the top of the leaves that the attas carry and keep watch. In the event of an enemy attack, they protect their friends, despite their small size.

Omar: That is another amazing example of self-sacrifice. But I want to know one more thing. What do attas use these leaves for? Why do attas keep carrying those leaves all day long?

The Ant: They need them for their farming. Attas use these leaves to grow fungus. Ants cannot eat the leaves themselves. So, worker ants make a heap of these pieces of leaves after chewing them, and then place them in the underground chambers in their nest. In these chambers, they grow fungus on the leaves and

obtain their food from the shoots of the growing fungus.

You must now be wondering how tiny ants can carry out such miraculous events all by themselves?

Omar: Yes. I am really trying to understand how ants manage to do all that. For example, if you asked me to grow fungus, it would not be at all easy for me to do. At the very least, I would have to read some books or else seek the advice of people who do know how to do it. But I know that attas do not receive any training like this.

Now I can better understand what makes you and your ant friends so talented. You are programmed to do your jobs.

For example, attas come into the world already knowing about farming. Certainly, God, the Creator of all living things, gave attas this skill. It is God Who created you and all your friends with all these awesome features.

The Ant: You are right, Omar. We know all these things innately. Our Creator, God, gave them to us as blessings.

Omar was late again. He thanked him, and left for school. As he walked, the things his ant friend had told him were still echoing in his ears. Meanwhile, he kept on thinking.

Ants' skilful actions pointed to a great wisdom. But this wisdom could not belong to the ants themselves. They were, after all, tiny creatures. Then all ants' skills must show man the wisdom of God. In order to show the greatness of His being and His art of creation, God, the Creator of the ants, made these tiny creatures carry out tasks they could never do by their own wisdom and will.

His friend owed his innate wisdom, skill and sacrificing nature to the inspiration of God. Everything he did was proof not of his, but of God's power and wisdom.

Thinking about all that, he realized that certain things that he had earlier imagined differently had been replaced by true versions of the facts. He understood once again that the stories told about living things, how they came into existence by chance, how they acquired the skills they had by chance over periods of time, were lies. How could they be true? Just think, how could ants "talk" to each other so perfectly if they had come into being by chance? How could they make contact with each other without any disorder, and build perfect nests? Besides, even if all these ants had come into existence by chance and if they lived only to defend themselves, how was it that they could make such enormous sacrifices for one another?

He thought about these things all day at school. When he got home in the evening, he

Attas carrying the leaves they have cut.

decided to read the Qur'an, which God sent down to all people. The first verse he read was the following:

In the creation of the heavens and the earth, and the alternation of night and day, there are Signs for people with intelligence: those who remember God, standing, sitting and lying on their sides, and reflect on the creation of the heavens and the earth (by saying): 'Our Lord, You have not created this for nothing. Glory be to You! So safeguard us from the punishment of the Fire.' (Surah Al Imran: 190-191)

He was totally convinced that God alone created the ant, himself, his mother and father, his brother and everything in the universe. His little friend had reminded him of the most important fact in the world: that there was no creator but God.

I believe that when you read these lines, all of you

He told a lie

will also understand the truth like Omar, and know that it is God Who created everything. Then you will say: "Darwin, who said that 'living beings were not created, but came into existence by chance' was a big liar. When we are surrounded by creatures with so many fascinating skills, it is impossible to think that they came into existence by chance."

So, if like Omar you also chance upon a good friend one day, never forget that you have a lot to learn from him. Investigate and think about the perfection in the art of God, Who created him. And if you ever meet liars like Darwin, tell them about the features of your little friends and say that you will never ever believe in their nonsensical lies.

Goodword kidz

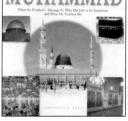

Tell Me About
HAJJ
What the Hajj Is, Why It's So Important and What It Teaches Me

LIFE BEGINS
Quran Stories for Little Hearts

THE BRAVE BOY
Quran Stories for Little Hearts

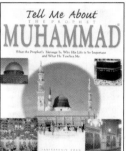

Tell Me About
THE PROPHET
MUHAMMAD
What the Prophet's Message Is, Why His Life Is So Important and What He Teaches Me

THE FIRST MAN
Quran Stories for Little Hearts

THE TWO BROTHERS
Quran Stories for Little Hearts

THE ARK OF NUH
Quran Stories for Little Hearts

ALLAH'S BEST FRIEND
Quran Stories for Little Hearts

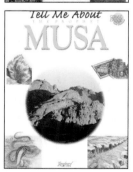

Tell Me About
THE PROPHET
MUSA

Children's Stories from the Quran
The Ark of Nuh
and the Great Flood
Sticker Book

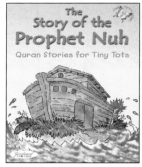

The
Story of the
Prophet Nuh
Quran Stories for Tiny Tots

The Blessings of
RAMADAN

Javed Ali

THE STORY OF THE PROPHET YUSUF

HONEYBEES
THAT BUILD PERFECT COMBS

HARUN YAHYA

goodwordkidz